Mia,

please use this
to write your thoughts,
dreams etc. As I give this
to you to use, I will also begin
writing in my journal. Hopefully
journal writing will be good [n ?]
I miss you and hope to see you soon

Peace & love,

Liv 1/00

*O*UR TRUE HOME
IS IN THE PRESENT MOMENT. WHEN WE ENTER THE
PRESENT MOMENT DEEPLY, OUR REGRETS AND SORROWS DISAPPEAR,
AND WE DISCOVER LIFE WITH ALL ITS WONDERS.

*W*riting in a journal can help us become more aware of ourselves and more present to what is happening around us. In the pages of this journal, Thich Nhat Hanh's simple, yet profound messages about life can provide guidance and inspiration along the way.

Thich Nhat Hanh *is a poet, Zen master and peace activist. The author of thirty-five books, he was nominated by Martin Luther King for the Nobel Peace Prize. In exile from his native Vietnam since 1966, he lives in Plum Village, the meditation community he founded in southwestern France.*

The Five Awarenesses

One

We are aware that all generations of our ancestors and all future generations
are present in us.

Two

We are aware of the expectations that our ancestors, our children
and their children have of us.

Three

We are aware that our joy, peace, freedom and harmony are the joy, peace,
freedom and harmony of our ancestors, our children and their children.

Four

We are aware that understanding is the very foundation of love.

Five

We are aware that blaming and arguing never help us and only create a
wider gap between us, that only understanding,
trust and love can help us change and grow.

If you love someone,

the greatest gift you

can give them is

your presence.

By making

peace with our

parents,

 in us

we have a

chance to make

real peace with

ourselves.

THE RHYTHM OF MY HEART IS THE BIRTH
AND DEATH OF ALL THAT IS ALIVE.

Please make yourself into
someone we can rely on.

Follow your breathing,
dwell mindfully on
your steps, and soon
you will find your
balance. Visualize a
tiger walking slowly,
and you will find that
your steps become as
majestic as hers.

People say that walking on water is a miracle;
but to me, walking peacefully on Earth
is the real miracle.

I HAVE ARRIVED

   I AM HOME

IN THE HERE,

      IN THE NOW.

I AM SOLID.

   I AM FREE.

   IN THE ULTIMATE I DWELL.

When we
enter the
present
moment
deeply, our
regrets and
sorrows
disappear,
and we
discover life
with all its
wonders.

Bring the earth your love
and happiness.
The earth will
be safe when
we feel safe
in ourselves.

WE

DON'T

RUSH

TO THE

FUTURE

BECAUSE

WE KNOW

THAT

EVERYTHING

IS HERE

IN THE

PRESENT

MOMENT.

Walking in mindfulness
brings us peace and joy,
and makes our life real.
Why rush? Our final
destination will only
be the graveyard.

Why not walk in the
direction of life, enjoying
peace in each moment
with every step?

In daily life, there is so much to
do and so little time. You
may feel pressured to
run all the time.
Just stop! Touch the
ground of the present
moment deeply, and you
will touch peace and joy.

Each moment
you are alive is a gem,

shining through  and containing Earth

and sky,

and clouds.

You, the richest person on Earth,

who have been going around begging,

stop being the destitute child.

Come back and claim your heritage.

Enjoy your happiness and offer it to everyone.

The tears I shed yesterday
have become rain.

Breathing in,
I am a mountain,
imperturbable,
still,
alive,
rigorous,
Breathing out,
I feel solid,
The waves of emotion
can never carry me away.

AS WE CULTIVATE PEACE AND

HAPPINESS IN OURSELVES,

WE ALSO NOURISH PEACE AND

HAPPINESS IN THOSE WE LOVE.

When the mind settles on the mountain,

it becomes the mountain.

WHAT IS MOST IMPORTANT IS TO FIND
PEACE AND TO SHARE IT WITH OTHERS.

It is only when
you realize that peace
and happiness are available
here in the present moment

that you will be able to relax.

MINDFULNESS IS THE LIGHT THAT SHOWS US THE WAY.

WE ARE

VERY MUCH

A CONTINUATION

OF OUR PARENTS

AND OUR ANCESTORS.

TO BE ANGRY AT OUR PARENTS

IS TO BE ANGRY AT OURSELVES.

TO RECONCILE WITH OUR PARENTS IS TO

MAKE PEACE WITH

OURSELVES.

QUOTES IN THIS JOURNAL ARE FROM THE FOLLOWING BOOKS BY
THICH NHAT HANH, PUBLISHED BY PARALLAX PRESS:

Call Me By My True Names

A Joyful Path

The Sun My Heart

The Long Road Turns to Joy

For more information about Thich Nhat Hanh, his books and tapes, and a
complete schedule of his retreats and lectures, contact Parallax Press/Community
of Mindful Living, P.O. Box 7355, Berkeley, CA 94707. www.parallax.org

Photography: Ed Brown

Journal Design: Tarane' Sayler

Brush Dance

For more information about Brush Dance, or to find out where to purchase
our cards, journals and other products, contact us at
100 Ebbtide Avenue, Bldg. #1, Sausalito, CA 94965 415 331 9030.
www.brushdance.com

Printed in Korea